Blue Mind for Dummies

The World's Simplest Guide to Your
Two Most Powerful Brain Colours

DR. ARPIT BANSAL

The Aquaman Biohacker

Cancer Surgeon · Longevity Expert · Gut-Brain Specialist

notionpress.com

INDIA • SINGAPORE • MALAYSIA

ISBN 979-8-90451-928-5

For Aarna.

My daughter. My reason.

I named you Aarna. In Hindi mythology, Aarna means flowing water. The river that never stops. The ocean that never fears. The water that finds its way, always.

I did not understand why I was so drawn to that name until I began writing about Blue Mind — about the nervous system, about water, about going with the flow, about trusting the tide. And then I realised: you were always the living proof of this way of life.

Your name is the entire message of this book.

A major credit for the idea behind this book goes to you, Aarna — because your name, meaning flowing water, is where my life's purpose became clear. You taught your Dada the most important lesson: flow is not something you chase. It is something you already are.

May you always know your colour. May you always go with the flow.

— Dada

And for every person in the world —
young or old, calm or anxious, healing or thriving —
this book is for you too.

Preface

Why a book this simple had to exist.

There are thousands of books on stress, anxiety, sleep, performance, and longevity. Most of them are heavy. Most of them require you to be a certain kind of reader — educated, patient, already healthy enough to absorb a hundred pages of theory before a single tool reaches your nervous system. That is a problem.

The people who need this information the most are not sitting in libraries. They are in hospital waiting rooms. In classrooms. In traffic. In kitchens at 2 a.m. with a crying child. On their tenth hour of Zoom calls. On an oncology ward holding a hand. On a phone, scrolling through yet another notification that their body reads as a threat.

This book is for them. For a six-year-old who can't explain why her chest feels tight. For a thirteen-year-old who can't sleep. For a sixty-three-year-old who powered through for decades and is now being told — by his own body — that the bill has come due.

> *"The simplest truths about the human nervous system are the ones we most urgently need to hear — and the ones science has made most unreadable."*

I wrote a longer, technical book called The Blue Mind Code for doctors, scientists, and serious biohackers. This is not that book. This book contains the same science, stripped of jargon, translated into a language any human being can use on the same day they read it. If there is a word that needs a scientist's explanation, it is marked with a star (†) and explained in the Go with the Flow Glossary — your decoder ring.

Read this book front to back if you like. Or flip to any chapter. Or read one page to your child at bedtime. Or share a single paragraph at a family dinner.

This is not a textbook.
It is a transmission.
And the world needs it now.

Go with the Flow.

— Dr. Arpit Bansal, The Aquaman Biohacker

Contents

CHAPTER 1

Your Brain Has Two Colours

You only need two colours to understand your entire nervous system.

Imagine your brain is a light switch. But instead of ON and OFF, it has two colours: RED and BLUE. That's it. That's the whole secret. Two halves, two jobs. One switch you can learn to flip. Your entire nervous system † — the invisible wiring that controls how you feel, how you think, how you heal, how you sleep, how you love — runs on just these two colours. Your nervous system has only TWO colours. Blue and Red. The most important skill in life is knowing which one you're in — and how to change it. Most people go through their entire lives never knowing these two colours exist. They feel stressed, anxious, and exhausted — but they don't know why. They feel calm, creative, and happy sometimes — but they don't know how to get back there. This book teaches you both. Let's start by understanding each colour properly. Know your colour. Choose your colour.

Go with the Flow Glossary

Nervous system†: The body's electrical wiring — brain, spinal cord, and nerves that control everything you feel, think, and do.

Sympathetic†: The 'speed up' branch — activates Red Mind.

Parasympathetic†: The 'slow down' branch — activates Blue Mind.

CHAPTER 2

RED MIND — The Colour of Alarm

The fire inside you that saves your life — until it doesn't.

Red Mind is not a bad thing. It is a SURVIVAL thing. Millions of years ago, when our ancient ancestors were out in the wild, they needed to survive. Lions. Tigers. Danger everywhere. When a lion appeared, the brain needed to act FAST. Here is the problem: your brain cannot tell the difference between a lion chasing you and a deadline, an angry email, an argument, a scary news headline, or a maths test. To your brain, all of those things feel like a lion. So it turns on Red Mind. The emergency alarm. Your heart races. Your breathing gets short. You can't think clearly. You can't sleep properly. Your gut hurts. You feel tired but can't rest. And here is the really important part: most people in today's world are in Red Mind almost ALL DAY — not just for three minutes (like with a real lion), but for sixteen hours straight. Every. Single. Day.

What Red Mind Feels Like (At Any Age)

- Heart beating fast for no physical reason
- Jaw clenched, shoulders hunched up near your ears
- Breathing from your chest, short and fast
- Stomach tight, queasy, or uncomfortable
- Mind going around in circles on the same worry
- Feeling like you are always behind, always rushing
- Waking up tired even after sleeping
- Getting annoyed easily at small things
- Feeling like you CANNOT stop — even when you want to

Name the Red. It loses its power.

Go with the Flow Glossary

Amygdala†: Your brain's alarm bell — triggers fear and Red Mind responses.

Cortisol†: The body's main stress chemical. A little is useful; too much damages your brain, gut, and immune system.

HPA Axis†: The stress alarm system — like a fire alarm that sometimes gets stuck ON.

Fight-or-flight†: The Red Mind survival response — fight danger or run from it.

Chapter 2

CHAPTER 3

BLUE MIND — The Colour of Calm

The water inside you that heals everything.

It is the state your body goes to when it feels safe. When it knows the lion is gone. When it can finally do what it was designed to do: heal, grow, repair, create, love, and thrive.

What Your Body Does in Blue Mind

- Heart beats slowly and powerfully — efficiently
- Blood pressure comes down to healthy levels
- Digestion switches ON — gut absorbs nutrients properly
- Immune system activates — your body can fight illness
- Cells start repairing damage from the day
- Sleep becomes deep and truly restorative
- Creativity flows — new ideas come easily
- You feel calm AND alert at the same time
- You can think clearly and make wise decisions

The vagus nerve † is the most important nerve you've probably never heard of. It runs from your brain all the way down through your heart, lungs, and gut. It is the physical cable of Blue Mind. When it is buzzing — you are in Blue Mind. When it goes quiet, you slide toward Red. Mind IS this system being in charge.

Why Water Activates Blue Mind So Powerfully

This is the Aquaman Biohacker's greatest discovery: water is the fastest, most powerful switch to Blue Mind that exists on Earth. When you are near water — the ocean, a river, a swimming pool, even a long shower — your nervous system recognises something ancient. Something that says: safe. The mammalian diving reflex † fires. Your heart rate drops. Your vagus nerve activates. Your brain shifts colour from Red to Blue almost instantly. This is not poetry. This is biology. And it works for every human being on the planet, at every age. Blue Mind is not a mood. It is not a luxury. It is the biological state your body is designed to live in. Blue is not calm. Blue is alive.

Go with the Flow Glossary

Vagus nerve†: A super-long nerve from brain to belly. The Blue Mind highway — when active, you feel calm, safe, and creative.

Parasympathetic†: The 'rest and repair' team. The opposite of fight-or-flight.

Default mode network†: Lights up when you daydream, imagine, get creative. Comes fully alive in Blue Mind.

Mammalian diving reflex†: Face touches cool water → heart slows → instant calm.

Chapter 3

CHAPTER 4

The One Rule That Changes Everything

The simplest test you'll ever learn.

Here is the most important idea in this entire book. Read it slowly. Red Mind should only be used for things you CAN DO SOMETHING ABOUT — right now. That's the whole rule. Let's unpack it. Red Mind exists for action. For response. For doing something. It is useful when there is a problem you can solve RIGHT NOW.

The Three Categories of Things

The Past — Something happened last week. Someone said something that hurt you. You made a mistake. Can you change the past? No. Not one second of it. Being in Red Mind about something that has already happened does NOTHING to change it. It only damages your body and your mood today. The Future — Something might happen next month. Or next year. Or maybe never. Your brain is imagining worst-case scenarios. For a future event that hasn't happened yet — and that you CANNOT control right now — Red Mind does nothing helpful. You are spending real energy, real health, real cellular damage on a problem that is entirely imaginary. The Present — There is something happening RIGHT NOW that needs your action. A fire to put out. A decision to make. A physical emergency. This is the ONLY valid use of Red Mind. Do it. Act. Solve. Then return to Blue. The only moment worth your Red Mind energy is the one where you can actually DO something. For everything else — BLUE is your home. Ask. Act. Then come home.

Go with the Flow Glossary

Prefrontal cortex†: The 'thinking brain' — helps you pause, reflect, and choose your response.

Default mode network†: The brain's resting state — active during daydreaming and Blue Mind.

Chapter 4

CHAPTER 5

The Purple Zone — Where Life Happens

Where Blue meets Red. Where you come alive.

. Pure Blue Mind — 100% calm and still — is deep sleep. Beautiful and necessary. But you can't live your whole day there. Pure Red Mind — 100% alarm — is panic. Also necessary, very occasionally. But terrible as a permanent address. Most of real, rich, joyful human life happens in the space BETWEEN the two. In the Purple zone. Blue is your home. Purple is where most of life happens. Blue is the main magic colour. It is your foundation, your home base, the state your body is designed to live in most of the time. Purple is what happens when you add just the right amount of Red to your Blue base — like an artist mixing paint.

The Blue Mind Colour Spectrum

BLUE MIND — 100% Blue

Deep sleep, Yoga Nidra, flotation tank, deep meditation. Beautiful. Restorative. Necessary.

BLUISH PURPLE — 90% Blue + 10% Red

Morning journaling, gentle swim, creative writing, slow yoga, deep reading, a long walk with a friend. Your best creative and connection work.

MID PURPLE — 80% Blue + 20% Red

Runner's high, deep focus work, surgical flow state, teaching, delivering a passionate talk. The optimal zone for most high-performance activities.

REDDISH PURPLE — 60% Blue + 40% Red

Competitive sport, intense exercise, high-stakes presentation, excited creativity. Approaching the Red boundary but still productive.

RED MIND — 100% Red

Panic attack, rage, acute emergency. Body in full survival mode. Zero healing, zero creativity, zero wise decision-making. The goal is never to stay at one end. The goal is Blue as your HOME — your default, your resting state — and to visit Red and Purple consciously, by choice, when the moment calls for it. Then return home. Life is purple. Navigate it.

Go with the Flow Glossary

Flow state†: Complete absorption — time disappears, performance peaks.

Purple Zone†: The productive spectrum between Blue and Red.

Chapter 5

CHAPTER 6

Flow State — The Sweetest Spot

The place where time disappears and you become what you do.

Have you ever been so absorbed in something that you forgot time existed? Playing a sport. Drawing. Coding. Cooking. Dancing. Playing music. Having a great conversation. Reading the perfect book. Time disappears. Worry disappears. You are completely, totally, beautifully HERE. In Flow, the worrying mind takes a nap. You become the doing. That is Flow State †. And it lives in the Purple zone. Flow is always a shade of Blue — because Blue Mind is its foundation. But Flow needs a little Red mixed in for energy and focus. That's why Flow lives in the Purple zone — it's mostly Blue with just enough Red to make it come alive.

Flow Is Different for Every Person, Every Moment

Here is the beautiful thing: your Flow shade of purple can be different every time. A surgeon in the operating theatre might be at 80% Blue, 20% Red. A surfer catching a big wave might be at 60% Blue, 40% Red. A child lost in drawing might be at 90% Blue, 10% Red. Same person, different activities, different days — different shades of purple. And that is perfectly normal. Your Flow blend is as unique as your fingerprint, and it can shift depending on what you are doing and how you are feeling that day. Think of a runner: some days the flow comes at kilometre five, some days at kilometre twelve. Some days it's a gentle, dreamy Bluish Purple. Other days it's a powerful, intense Mid Purple. Both are Flow. Both are beautiful. Both are always a shade of the Blue.

How to Invite Flow

- Choose something that is slightly challenging — not too easy, not too hard
- Remove distractions — especially your phone
- Start from a place of calm (Blue Mind is the foundation)
- Give it at least 15–20 minutes before it clicks
- Trust that it will come — don't force it

Flow cannot be forced. It can only be invited. And the best invitation is always a calm, Blue Mind base. Find your purple. Flow finds you.

Go with the Flow Glossary

Dopamine†: The reward chemical — released during flow and achievement.

Transient hypofrontality†: When the thinking brain quiets down — allowing flow.

CHAPTER 7

How to Go Blue — Fast

Practical tools for every age, every moment.

Here is the beautiful truth: your nervous system can be switched from Red to Blue in seconds. Not hours. Not days. Seconds. Your breath is the fastest, most direct dial you have. Because breathing is the ONLY part of your nervous system that runs automatically AND can be controlled manually. When you consciously change your breathing, you change your colour. The Blue Breath: four in, four hold, four out, four hold.

Tool 1: The Blue Breath (Box Breathing)

Breathe in for 4 counts. Hold for 4 counts. Breathe out for 4 counts. Hold for 4 counts. Repeat 4 times. Used by surgeons, Navy SEALs, Olympic athletes, and now — you.

Tool 2: Cold Water on Your Face

Splash cold water on your face. Hold it there for 30 seconds. This triggers the mammalian diving reflex † — an ancient biological response that tells your brain you are entering water. Heart rate drops. Vagus nerve fires. Blue Mind activates. Instantly. This works for adults and children equally.

Tool 3: Humming

Hum a single note. Keep humming on your exhale. The vibration directly activates the vagus nerve through your throat and chest. Nitric oxide † is released in the sinuses. Immediate calming. Children love this one — make it into a game.

Tool 4: Go Near Water

The ocean. A river. A lake. A fountain. A bathtub. Even the sound of water on your phone. Your brain recognises water as safe. Your parasympathetic nervous system activates. Blue Mind descends on you like a wave of calm. Free. Available everywhere. More powerful than most medicines.

Tool 5: Underwater Meditation

Go beneath the surface — in a pool, the ocean, even a deep bathtub. Float. Let the water hold you. Close your eyes and breathe slowly through your snorkel, or simply hold your breath gently. The combination of hydrostatic pressure †, sensory simplification, and the diving reflex creates the deepest Blue Mind state available to the human body. Nothing on land can match it. This is the Aquaman Biohacker's signature practice.

Tool 6: Panoramic Vision

Instead of focusing on one point, widen your gaze. Look at the whole room. Let your peripheral vision expand. This signals safety to your brain — you are not hunting, not being hunted. Just being. Blue Mind activates.

Tool 7: The Slow Walk

Walk slowly. Not like you are going somewhere. Like you are already there. No phone. No earphones. Just walking. Feel the ground. Notice your breath. Two minutes of this shifts the nervous system colour measurably. Breathe. Splash. Hum. You're home.

Go with the Flow Glossary

Box breathing†: Inhale 4 counts, hold 4, exhale 4, hold 4. Activates the vagus nerve.

Mammalian dive reflex†: Cold water on face → instant calm, heart rate drops.

Nitric oxide†: Relaxes blood vessels and calms the brain. Humming makes more of it.

CHAPTER 8

Water — The Blue Mind Superpower

The oldest medicine on earth is not a pill. It is a river.

Of all the tools to access Blue Mind, water is the most ancient, the most powerful, and the most underused. Wallace J. Nichols — the marine biologist who first named Blue Mind — showed that being near, in, or around water produces a measurably calmer, more creative, more connected brain state. One drop, endless ripples. This is what water does inside you. As a surgeon, here is WHY it works

- The Mammalian Diving Reflex: Even just seeing water signals to your ancient brain — 'enter safe, slow mode'. Heart rate drops. Vagus nerve fires.
- Hydrostatic Pressure: Water touching your skin sends a full-body signal of safety. Like a whole-body hug.
- Breath Control: Swimming forces you to breathe rhythmically and consciously. Controlled breathing IS vagal activation.
- Sensory Simplification: Underwater, the complex world quiets. Your default mode network † — your creative, restorative brain network — comes fully online.
- Negative Ions †: Ocean air and moving water produce negative ions that increase serotonin † (your calm-happiness chemical) in the brain.

Water is not just pleasant. It is medicinal. It is the oldest Blue Mind pharmacy on Earth. And it is free. When you have enough, you feel content and peaceful. Most of it is made in your gut.

Water Practices for All Ages

- Swim in the ocean, a lake, a pool — anywhere you can
- Take a long shower with eyes closed, feeling the water
- Sit by any body of water for 10 minutes with no phone
- Listen to water sounds (rain, waves, rivers) before sleep
- Practice underwater meditation — the deepest Blue

Mind

- Splash cold water on your face when stressed (instant reset)
- Walk in the rain — let your nervous system remember
- Float — in a pool, a bath, a flotation tank

Water never forgets your rhythm.

Go with the Flow Glossary

Blue space†: Any environment near water — oceans, rivers, lakes, baths.

Negative ions†: Molecules near moving water — improve mood and calm.

Hydrostatic pressure†: Water's gentle squeeze signals safety to your nervous system.

Chapter 8

CHAPTER 9

For Little Ones (Ages 4–12)

How to teach your child something most adults never learn.

Children feel their colours more naturally than adults do. They haven't yet learned to pretend they're not in Red Mind. When a child is scared, sad, or overwhelmed — they show you. That's actually a gift. The long exhale of a bubble blow is the vagus nerve's favourite game.

The Body Scan for Kids

Ask your child: "Where do you feel it in your body right now?" Show them that the tight chest, the stomach ache, the racing heart — that's just Red Mind visiting. And it will leave. Because Blue Mind is always waiting.

Blue Mind Activities for Children

- Swimming and splashing in water (the #1 tool for all ages)
- Blowing bubbles — the long exhale activates the vagus nerve
- Humming a song together
- Slow, mindful drawing or colouring
- Star breathing: arms wide on inhale, arms folded on exhale
- Lying in the grass and watching clouds
- Reading any of your favourite books before sleep (not just calming ones — any book you love)
- Playing in nature without a destination
- Underwater meditation in a pool (with a parent nearby): floating, eyes closed, feeling the water hold you

A Note for Parents

The most powerful thing you can do for your child's nervous system is to regulate YOUR OWN first. Children are biological mirrors. When you are in Red Mind — anxious, rushing, tense — they feel it in their own nervous systems, even when you haven't said a word. Your Blue Mind is your greatest parenting tool. The child who knows their colours grows into an adult who never loses themselves. Teach them young. They'll flow forever.

Go with the Flow Glossary

Co-regulation†: A calm adult's nervous system helps calm a child's.

Window of tolerance†: The zone where a child can handle stress without losing control.

Chapter 9

CHAPTER 10

For Teenagers (Ages 13–19)

The hardest years. The most important colours.

. Teenagers have the most turbulent nervous systems of any age group on earth. This is not a character flaw. It is biology. The prefrontal cortex † — the brain's wise, calm decision-making centre — is not fully developed until age 25. The amygdala † — the brain's alarm centre — is running at full power from puberty. This means teenagers feel things at maximum intensity, with minimum braking. Red side — scrolling. Blue side — the exit. Both live in the same brain.

The Teenage Red Mind Traps

- Social media: every notification is a tiny stress alarm to your brain
- Sleep deprivation: the #1 cause of teenage Red Mind — screens at night destroy it
- Academic pressure: the threat of failure = brain = lion chasing
- Social comparison: comparing yourself to everyone online = permanent Red Mind
- No recovery time: always doing, never just being

Blue Mind Practices for Teenagers

- Morning cold shower — 30 seconds. Brutal and brilliant.

Changes the whole day.

- Phone-free time before sleep — minimum 30 minutes
- Reading any book you love before bed — not just

'calming' ones, any favourite

- One physical activity that puts you in flow: sport, dance, music, martial arts
- Swimming, wherever possible — the ultimate nervous system reset
- Journaling — 5 minutes, no rules, just write

- Underwater meditation: even just floating face-down with a snorkel for 5 minutes
- Time in nature — the single most underrated Blue Mind tool

You don't need more hours of productivity. You need better quality recovery. Blue Mind is not laziness. Blue Mind is the thing that makes everything else possible. Feel it all. Then find your Blue.

Go with the Flow Glossary

Prefrontal pruning†: Teenage brain under construction — thinking brain not fully wired until 25.

Limbic system†: The emotional brain — fully active in teens, often overriding thinking.

Amygdala†: The brain's alarm bell — extra loud in teenagers.

Chapter 10

CHAPTER 11

For Adults

The ones who forgot how to come home.

Adults have a unique problem: they have learned to suppress the Red Mind signals. Instead of noticing the tight jaw, the shallow breath, the restless sleep — they just power through. They call it resilience. I call it a ticking clock. As a cancer surgeon, I have operated on thousands of adults who powered through for years — and eventually, the body sent a much louder message.

The Adult Blue Mind Protocol — Daily

- Morning: Before checking your phone — 5 breaths.

Slow. Deep. Blue first.

- Midday: 3-minute walk, phone in pocket, eyes wide open. Panoramic vision.
- Before difficult conversations: box breathing, 5 cycles.
- After work: a transition ritual — shower, swim, walk, or music. Signal to your brain: work is done.
- Evening: screens off 30 minutes before sleep. Read any book you enjoy. The night belongs to Blue Mind.

The HRV Check

Heart Rate Variability † (HRV) is the best way to measure your Blue Mind in real time. It measures the tiny variation between heartbeats. High HRV = Blue Mind. Low HRV = Red Mind. Most modern smartwatches measure this. Track it. It tells you the truth about your nervous system when your mind is too busy to notice. Your Blue Mind is your greatest parenting tool. Your Blue Mind is also your greatest leadership tool, relationship tool, and longevity tool. Stop powering through. Power down.

Go with the Flow Glossary

Allostatic load†: Cumulative cost of chronic stress — the 'bill' that comes due.

HRV†: Heart Rate Variability — more variation = healthier nervous system.

Burnout†: When Red Mind becomes the default — exhaustion and disconnection.

Chapter 11

CHAPTER 12

The Daily Colour Check-In

Your five-question tool. Use it every day.

Do this three times a day. Morning, midday, evening. It takes 30 seconds.

STOP

Pause whatever you are doing.

SCAN

What colour am I right now? Red, Purple, or Blue? What percentage blend?

ASK

Does this moment actually require this colour?

SHIFT

If not, what is ONE thing I can do in the next 3 minutes to change?

The Blue Mind Decision Tree

Whenever you feel stressed, anxious, upset, or overwhelmed, ask yourself: "Am I in Red Mind right now — and does this moment actually require it?" If YES — act. Solve. Then return to Blue. If NO — use any Blue Mind tool. Breathe. Splash water. Hum. Walk. Go near water. Come home. The past is done. The future is not here. The only

moment that is real is now. And in this moment — you can always choose Blue. Notice. Name. Navigate. Repeat.

Go with the Flow Glossary

Interoception†: Sensing what's happening inside your body — a key Blue Mind skill.

Self-regulation†: Managing your own nervous system state — choosing Blue over Red.

Chapter 12

CHAPTER 13

What You Now Know That Most People Don't

Everything you need, in one place.

You have just read something that most human beings live an entire lifetime without learning.

- Your nervous system runs on two colours. Blue and Red.
- Blue Mind is your biological home — your healing, creating, connecting state.
- Red Mind is for action — not for worry about things that have already happened or might never happen.
- The one rule: only stay in Red Mind when you can DO something right now.
- Water is the most powerful Blue Mind switch on earth.
- The tools — breathing, cold water, humming, slow walks, nature, underwater meditation.
- Flow lives in the Purple zone, always a shade of Blue — and requires Blue as its foundation.
- Blue is the main magic colour. Everything beautiful starts from Blue.
- Your Blue Mind is your greatest parenting tool — and your greatest living tool.

The One Practice

Three times a day, ask yourself: What colour am I in? If you don't need Red — choose Blue. That's it. Your nervous system is trainable. It is never too late. It works for everyone at every age. You do not need any equipment, any money, or any special talent. You only need a willingness to notice, and a choice to come home. Come home to Blue.

Go with the Flow Glossary

Blue Mind†: Your parasympathetic healing state — calm, creative, connected.

Red Mind†: Your sympathetic alarm state — useful for action, harmful when chronic.

Purple Zone†: The productive middle — enough Red activation with a Blue foundation.

If You Loved This Book —

what to read, hear, and join next.

Go Deeper · The Blue Mind Code

If what you have just read lit something up in you — if you want the science behind every chapter, the deeper protocols, the surgical detail on the vagus nerve, the HPA axis, the gut–brain axis, the underwater meditation practice, and the biohacking architecture of a Blue Mind life — my companion book The Blue Mind Code is written for you. It is the scientist's edition of this book. Same philosophy. Ten times the depth.

Coming Soon · The Purple Book

The Purple Zone deserves a book of its own — and it is being written. High performance without high cost. Flow as a daily instrument. The science of living a Mid-Purple life without slipping into Red. Watch this space.

Join the Movement · #GoWithTheFlow

The Blue Mind movement began with Wallace J. Nichols and continues to grow. It is not a brand. It is a quiet rebellion against a world that has forgotten how to rest. Every reader who practises Blue Mind, teaches a child their colours, or swims in the morning instead of scrolling is part of it. Share your Blue Mind moment and tag #GoWithTheFlow — every ripple matters.

Two Songs to Play While You Read This Book

♪ Blue Mind — Alexi Murdoch

The unofficial anthem of the Blue Mind movement. Dr. Wallace J. Nichols himself used this song as his iPhone alarm tone — the first sound of every morning. Three minutes of quiet that do what this book spends ninety pages trying to do.

Available on Spotify · Apple Music · YouTube

♪ Go With the Flow — Dr. Arpit Bansal

My own musical answer to the question this book asks. A song for the Purple Zone — for the diver and the surgeon, for the child and the grandparent, for anyone who is learning to stop paddling against the current of their own life.

Available on Spotify · Apple Music · YouTube

From the field

The rest of this book is simple.

It had to be.

Blue Mind needs to reach the people who would never pick up a paper on vagal tone or heart rate variability. So I wrote it the way water arrives at a thirsty mouth — without ceremony.

This one page is for something else.

This page is for my brother.

Dr. Harshit Bansal — Intervention Radiologist, co-author, quantum brother. My purpose was water. But it was he who brought me to it. He carried me to the edge of the tide before I had learned to listen to it. Everything blue in my life has a quiet hand beneath it, and the hand is his.

We are quantumly entangled water.

That is not metaphor. It is what we have lived. We have had moments beneath the surface where the boundary between his mind and mine — and the mind of an octopus, on different days, in different oceans — collapsed into one shared field. The same unified intelligence moving through two bodies of water on two ends of the earth, doing the exact same thing. And this is not a single instance. There have been more. They tend to arrive close to water, to nature, to earth.

He lives in the UK now. I stayed in India. By every clock and calendar, he is gone.

But on my daily run, there is a tree. One particular tree, and beside it two more, taller — standing close, the way two brothers stand. The day he flew out, I expected to feel his absence. I have not. Every time I pass those trees, I feel him there. Not in memory. In presence. Roots speaking to roots beneath the ground. Entanglement does not care about postcodes.

This is the part of Blue Mind that does not fit inside a Dummies book.

This is the part that lives beneath the language, beneath the science, beneath the tide.

The next book is already moving. Quantum Entangled Brothers — co-written with Harshit. The long-form expansion of this single page. The field made readable.

If this page caught you, the field is asking you to stay close.

trust the tide 🌊

— Dr. Arpit Bansal

For Harshit. Always.

The ocean always finds its way back to the shore.
So will you.

Go with the Flow.

— Dr. Arpit Bansal
The Aquaman Biohacker

About the Author

Dr. Arpit Bansal is a practising cancer surgeon, longevity expert, and gut-brain specialist. Known publicly as The Aquaman Biohacker, he is a lifelong daily swimmer who has spent his career operating at the intersection of surgical medicine and nervous system science – studying why some patients heal and some do not, and what the quiet state of the human nervous system has to do with the loudest outcomes in medicine.

He is the author of The Blue Mind Code, and a growing body of work that bridges the gap between clinical science and everyday practice. He lives, teaches, operates, writes, and swims – in that order on a good day, and in reverse on a better one.

For Aarna. My flowing water. My reason.

— Dada

www.ingramcontent.com/pod-product-compliance
Lightning Source LLC
LaVergne TN
LVHW051132210926
848482LV00001B/69
* 9 7 9 8 9 0 4 5 1 9 2 8 5 *